OLD-TIME RADIO MUSIC THEMES FOR UKULELE

by Dick Sheridan

To access audio visit:
www.halleonard.com/mylibrary

Enter Code
4892-8936-4403-4263

ISBN 978-1-57424-407-6
SAN 683-8022

Cover by James Creative Group

Copyright © 2021 CENTERSTREAM Publishing
P.O. Box 17878 - Anaheim Hills, CA 92817

www.centerstream-usa.com | centerstrm@aol.com | 714-779-9390

TABLE OF CONTENTS
Old-Time Radio Music Themes for Ukulele

List of Theme Songs 4

A Word from the Author 5

Classical Music Themes..6

Chart: Some Radio Shows with Classical Themes...7

Chart: Categories of Radio Shows 9

Commercials and Jingles...10

Chart: Name of Show, Dates Aired, Format, Program Length........................11

Premiums...12

Some Memorable Lines 13

Signature Songs 14

Chart: Radio Performers and Their Themes 14

On The Air...14

Low G Songs & Tuning...15

Chart: Radio Music Themes and Their Shows 16

Chart: Some Radio Shows and Their Music Themes 17

LIST OF THEME SONGS

A

April Showers 18

Arkansas Traveler 20

B

Believe Me If All Those Endearing Young Charms 22

Bury Me Not On the Lone Prarie 24

C

California, Here I Come 26

Charley My Boy 28

Columbia, the Gem of the Ocean 30

D

Darling Nelly Gray 32

E

Eyes of Texas, The 34

F

For He's A Jolly Good Fellow 36

Funiculi, Funicula 35

G

H

Hot Time in the Old Town Tonight 38

I

Ida! Sweet As Apple Cider 40

I've Been Working on the RR 42

J

Jimmy Crack Corn 39

Juanita 44

K

Kerry Dance, The 46

L

Love Nest 50

M

Memories 49

Merrily We Roll Along 52

My Wild Irish Rose 56

N

Nobody's Sweetheart 53

O

Oh! You Beautiful Doll 58

On the Trail of the Lonesome Pine 60

P

Piano Concerto, No. 1 62

Poor Butterfly 64

Pop! Goes the Weasel 66

R

Red River Valley 67

Rock-a-Bye Baby 68

Rose Room 70

S

School Days 72

Sidewalks of New York 74

Sunbonnet Sue 69

T

Toot, Toot, Tootsie 76

W

When Irish Eyes Are Smiling 80

Y

Yankee Doodle Boy 82

Year of Jubilo 79

A WORD FROM THE AUTHOR

The Golden Age of Radio

I admit it. I am a product of the radio generation. In my youth there was no television. Home entertainment was limited to the radio, phonograph, "parlor" piano, or occasionally to an 8mm silent film projector. But radio was king. It dominated.

My childhood home had several radios: an old console in the living room from the 1920s or 30s that had a distinctive smell when the dust-covered tubes heated up. Its green "cat's eye" dial tuned in different stations through static and squawks and a faint sound of distant telegraphs transmitting the dots and dashes of Morse code.

In my bedroom was a tiny crystal radio made from a kit. An antenna wire ran out the window to the garage roof, another wire led down to a pipe buried in the earth for a ground, and a set of army surplus earphones completed the assembly.

There was also a small radio by my bedside for late-night listening when homework was finished and bedtime loomed. Among the favorite programs were THE GREAT GILDERSLEEVES, DUFFY'S TAVERN, FIBBER McGEE & MOLLY, then the late night thrillers of SUSPENSE, INNER SANCTUM and LIGHTS OUT -- hardly the best shows for bringing peaceful slumber.

My Zenith bedside radio

My sister's ill-fated Emerson portable radio from the 1940s.

In the kitchen we had a small portable radio which provided the background for where most of our family gathered and where meals were usually taken. The radio had been a Christmas present to my sister. Excitedly Christmas morning she grabbed the radio and ran upstairs to show my parents who were still slumbering after having been up all night wrapping presents and putting them under the tree. She tripped on the stairs and the radio's case was shattered. My sister was devastated. But a replacement case was soon found, and the radio eventually found a permanent place on top of a kitchen cabinet.

That kitchen radio was seldom silent. It was the source of AUNT JENNEY'S REAL-LIFE STORIES for lunchtime school breaks and after-school children's shows like JACK ARMSTRONG, THE LONE RANGER, SGT. PRESTON OF THE YUKON and CAPTAIN MIDNIGHT. In the evening there was the humor of BABY SNOOKS, CORLISS ARCHER and HENRY ALDRICH. On the air Saturday night was the GRAND OLD OPREE, while Sunday afternoon for me was a highlight of listening: THE SHADOW with its sponsor of Blue Coal.

Sundays evenings were also special for the whole family and brought laughs at the dinner table and living room with JACK BENNY, CHARLIE McCARTHY, and FRED ALLEN and his "Allen's Alley" gang.

The impact of radio can't be overrated. Families were brought together in the shared experience of listening. Every home had at least one radio, often one in almost every room. Unlike television which requires visual attention, radio allowed the listener to do other things at the same time, Mom in the kitchen, Dad in the basement workshop, and the kids at play or doing their homework.

Different days and different times brought broadcasts that were special and eagerly awaited. Among my personal favorites was a New York City based program that ran week nights from 9:00 o'clock to midnight hosted by country music disk jockey and guitar-playing singer ROSALIE ALLEN. How I loved the recordings of her, Lulu Belle & Scotty, Homer & Jethro, and the popular country/western stars and rural singers of the day. Such shows led to a general appreciation of radio music, in all of its broad forms, and the thrust of the pages to follow.

Radio music began essentially in the early 1920s when the medium was in its infancy. Studios were primitive by today's standards: a microphone, a piano, a hand-cranked phonograph, and burlap sheets to muffle vibrations and baffle extraneous noises. The spoken word came later, but at first it was solely the classical music of phonograph recordings.

Live performances followed, initially with celebrated artists, often opera stars and their so-called "high brow" music. Popular performers and contemporary instrumental groups began to appear as "low brow" music was introduced. It was only natural that music in both forms -- high brow and low brow -- carried over as musical themes for emerging shows of the 1930s.

CLASSICAL MUSIC THEMES

For much of the listening audience, radio themes were their introduction to classical music. Many shows had musical directors who were well familiar with the field of classical music and could extract the perfect score for any given scene or situation. Of the shows that had multiple themes within the same broadcast, perhaps most noteworthy among them was THE LONE RANGER. Its principal theme was the overture to the opera "William Tell." Hidden within the show there were yet other classical extractions. Whenever there were Indians in the area, encamped or on the warpath, the Polovetsian Dances was introduced from Borodin's opera "Prince Igor." Children listening to the series probably had no idea they were listening to grand opera. Then as a finale for the show one more theme emerged: Franz Liszt's Les Preludes.

It is said that the mark of a truly knowledgeable fan of classical music is when the overture to "William Tell" is heard and can be identified by its proper name rather than as the theme for the LONE RANGER.

The list of radio shows with classical themes -- or classical sounding ones -- is extensive. Here are just a few examples:

SOME RADIO SHOWS WITH CLASSICAL THEMES

American School of the Air	Beethoven	Leonore Overture
American Weekly, The	Von Suppe	Light Cavalry Overture
Amos 'N' Andy	Breil	The Perfect Song
Bride and Groom	Wagner	Lohengrin, Wedding March
Buck Rogers	Liszt	Les Preludes
Captain Midnight	Wagner	Flying Dutchman Overture
Escape	Mussorgsky	Night On Bald Mountain
Family Hour	Debussy	Clair de Lune
Famous Jury Trials	Grieg	Ase's Death, Peer Gynt Suite
FBI in Peace and War	Prokofiev	Love for Three Oranges, March
Green Hornet, The	Rimsky-Korsakov	Flight of the Bumble Bee
Let's Pretend	Merchen und Volkskiedchen	Allegretto from Fairy Tales
Lone Ranger, The	Rossini	William Tell Overture
	Borodin	Polovetsian Dances
	Liszt	Les Preludes
Lorenzo Jones	Denza	Funiculi, Funicula
Mandrake, The Magician	Dukas	Sorcerer's Apprentice
Mercury Theater of the Air	Tchaikovsky	Piano Concerto No. 1
Metropolitan Opera Auditions	Wagner	Tannhauser Grand March
Mister District Attorney	Richard Strauss	Ein Heldenleben
Philip Morris Playhouse	Grophé	On The Trail, Grand Canyon Suite
Road of Life	Tchaikovsky	Pathetique Symphony No. 6
Sgt. Preston of the Yukon	Reznicek	Donna Diana Overture
Shadow, The	Saint-Saens	Omphale's Spinning Wheel
Today's Children	Johann Strauss	Tales from the Vienna Woods
We The People	Brahms	Symphony No. 1

For more than 40 of the world's most beautiful and enduring light classical masterpieces, see Centerstream's "Classical Music for the Ukulele."

Of course, not all music on the radio was theme music. Stations across the country would broadcast music independant of shows, music popular to their own region -- hillbilly, folk, country/western, easy listening, and national Top 40.

My mother was an avid fan of classical music. She was also a night owl who loved to sew well into the night with the radio softly on. Then as now there were few stations dedicated exclusively to classical music, but WQXR from New York was one. It had an all-night format, and from a small trapezoid-shaped red Emerson radio perched on top of her Martha Washington sewing cabinet, my mother would sew and listen to WQXR until the wee hours of the morning.

I always thought the dial of her radio and that of my bedside Zenith were reminiscent of the Trylon and Perisphere symbol of the 1939 NY World's Fair.

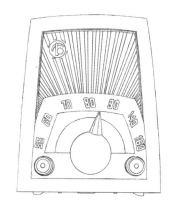

Along with the "classics" that descended from the early roots of radio music and the subsequent inclusion of contemporary popular songs, there also appeared **original scores** composed for the particular broadcast they introduced.

Most themes, incidentally, were instrumental without vocals. One exception was the children's talk and music show, UNCLE DON. Its theme was a spin-off of the song "Little Brown Jug" ...

Hello nephews, nieces too,

Mothers and daddies, how are you?

This is Uncle Don all set to go

With a meeting on the ra-di-o,

The father of a childhood friend was a radio script writer and producer. I recall his bringing my friend and me to one of his broadcasts. The format was probably typical of most shows at the time: voice actors standing around a microphone holding their scripts, a director in a control booth making hand signals, and an organ and organist providing the necessary theme, mood and scene transition music. It should be noted that throughout the golden radio years the organ was the principal provider of music for many shows.

A significant ingredient for certain shows was the use of **sound effects**. The individual or team providing these essentials had an array of noise makers that would boggle the mind if seen. Sounds were made of shoes walking, galloping horses, creaking doors , burning fires, thunder storms, screeching cars -- there seemed to be no limit to the array of gimmicks and noisy do-dads -- and the imaginative minds that created them.

Some shows had themes that would change over the years of the show's airing. **But not all shows had musical themes**. The WALTER WINCHELL news and gossip show, for example, had the sound of a pounding typewriter or telegraph key and Winchell's famous introduction: "Good evening Mr. and Mrs. America and all the ships at sea ..."

GANG BUSTERS, the crime/police show opened not with music but with the sound of police whistles, sirens, machine guns, breaking glass, screeching tires, and shuffling feet. TOWN HALL TONIGHT began with a town crier chanting **Oyez, Oyez!** Hear ye! Hear ye! Even a favorite children's show was deprived of a musical introduction, an announcer instead extolling the remarkable abilities of the show's hero with a background sound of rushing wind -- "It's a bird. It's a plane. It's SUPERMAN!" The HOP HARRIGAN show took off with the roar of an aircraft engine and "CX-4 calling control tower" as air ace Hop came in for a landing.

Let's take a look at the categories of most radio shows -- and a few examples of each. Some shows could run in length from 15 to 30 minutes, some special broadcasts like LUX RADIO THEATER and the MGM THEATER OF THE AIR ran a full 60 minutes.

CATEGORIES OF RADIO SHOWS

Children Action & Adventure	Let's Pretend; The Shadow; Captain Midnight; The Green Hornet; Superman; Dick Tracy; The Lone Ranger; Challenge of the Yukon
Comedy	The Bob Hope Show; Red Skelton Show; Bob and Ray; Lum and Abner
Adult Adventure	Escape; The Midnight Traveler
Horror & Suspense	Lights Out; Inner Sanctum; Suspense; The Whistler
News	Walter Winchell's Jergens Journal; H.V. Kaltenborn
Police & Detective	Mr. Keen, Tracer of Lost Persons; Gang Busters; FBI in Peace & War
Science Fiction	Dimension X (1950)
Serials	One Man's Family; The Light of the World
Situation Comedy (Sit Com)	Our Miss Brooks; The Great Gildersleeve; Fibber McGee and Molly; Duffy's Tavern; Phil Harris Alice Faye Show; The Life of Riley
Soap Operas	Stella Dallas; Backstage Wife; Today's Children; The Romance of Helen Trent; Road of Life; Ma Perkins
Sports	Special events with announcers Mel Allen, Red Barber, Bill Stern, et al.
Talk & Interviews	Mary Margaret McBride; Vox Pop

Variety	Arthur Godfrey Time; The Fred Waring Show; The Breakfast Club; The Dinah Shore Show; The Rudy Vallee Show; Major Bowes Original Amateur Hour
Western	Gene Autry's Melody Ranch; Death Valley Days; Tom Mix Ralston Straight Shooters; Gunsmoke
Quiz Shows	Quiz Kids; Information, Please; It Pay To Be Ignorant

COMMERCIALS & JINGLES

It wasn't long before advertisers realized the advantages of merchandising their wares to the vast audience of radio listeners. Commercials were introduced, sometimes woven into the actual plot of the show, sometimes in musical form used as a show's opening theme song.

In addition to the spoken word of commercials, short snatches of catchy music with clever lyrics were added to promote the program's sponsors. Enter the arrival of the JINGLE.

Looking good was the lure of many jingles, usually for skin and hair care products for the ladies, hair gel and shaving cream for the men. Cigarette companies were also major sponsors. Cheerful, lively commercials set to music promised taste, mildness and enjoyment with no throat irritation. Claims were made that there were no coughs "in a carload" along with the claim that of the tens of thousands of doctors who were polled one brand was preferred over another, the illusion being that tens of thousands of doctors actually smoked.

One TV commercial that appeared in 1948 just as radio was transitioning to television had cigarettes square dancing to an upbeat performance of *Turkey in the Straw*. Cigarette smoking was made to look like fun. Or so we were meant to believe.

Advertising agencies, together with song writers and composers, were working at full bore cranking out jingles that touted their clients products in creative and imaginative ways. Unfortunately, like original theme music, copyright laws prohibit the reproduction of these jingles in their musical form. However, with a little prowling on the Internet, a jingle can occasionally be heard in its entirety. For our purpose a hint of some of the more memorable jingles and their products can be found with a few lines of their jingles. Many of these jingles were the opening theme of the show whose product sponsored the show.

NAME OF SHOW - DATES AIRED - FORMAT - PROGRAM LENGTH

ABIE'S IRISH ROSE: (1942-1944), situation comedy, 30 min

ARTHUR GODFREY TIME: (1945-1972), talk, variety, music, 30 to 75 min

AUNT JENNY'S REAL-LIFE STORIES: (1937-1956), soap opera, 15 min.

BABY SNOOKS SHOW: (1936-1951), situation comedy, 30 min.

BOB BURNS SHOW: (1941-1949, regional humor, 30 min

BURL IVES SHOW: 1940-1949), folk songs, 15 min

BURNS & ALLEN SHOW: (1932-1950), situation comedy, 30 min

DAVID HARUM: 1936-1951) - soap opera, 15 min

DICK TRACY: (1934-1946), juvenile police series, 15-30 min

DON WINSLOW OF THE NAVY: (1937-1943) - juvenile adventure serials, 15 min.

DUFFY'S TAVERN: (1940-1952), situation comedy, 30 min

EDDIE CANTOR SHOW: (1931-1949), comedy/variety, 30 min

EDGAR BERGEN & CHARLIE McCARTHY SHOW: (1936-1955), comedy/variety, 30/60 min

GEORGE JESSEL SHOW: (1934-1938), comedy/variety, 30 min

HENRY MORGAN SHOW: (1940-1950), comedy, 15/30 min

HORN & HARDART CHILDREN'S HOUR: (1931-1957), juvenile variety, 30/60 min

JACK BENNY PROGRAM: (1932-1955) comedy, 30 min

JOAN DAVIS TIME: (1941-1950), comedy/variety, situation comedy, 30 min

JUST PLAIN BILL: (1932-1955), soap opera, 15 min

KRAFT MUSIC HALL: (1933-1949) variety, 60 min

LORENZO JONES: (1937-1955), comedy soap opera, 15 min

MERCURY THEATER OF THE AIR: (1938-1946), dramatic anthology, 30 min

MYRT & MARGE SHOW: (1931-1946), soap opera, 15 min

NATIONAL BARN DANCE: (1928-1949), country music, 30/60 min:

OUR GAL SUNDAY: (1937-1955), soap opera, 15 min

PHIL HARRIS & ALICE FAYE SHOW: (1946-1951), situation comedy, 30 min

PORTIA FACE LIFE: (1940-1951), soap opera, 15 min

QUIZ KIDS: (1940-1953), juvenile quiz show, 30 min

RAILROAD HOUR: (1948-1954), musical variety shows, 30/45 min

RED RYDER: (1942-1951), juvenile western series, 30 min

ROMANCE OF HELEN TRENT: (1933-1960), soap opera, 15 min

SPIKE JONES SHOW: (1945-1946), zany music, 30 min

STELLA DALLAS: (1937-1955), soap opera, 15 min

TALES OF THE TEXAS RANGERS: (1950-1952), western law & order, 30 min

TRUTH OR CONSEQUENCES: (1940-1956), gags & stunts, 30 min

VIC & SADE SHOW: (1932-1946), comedy series, 15 min

VOX POP: (1935-1948), interviews, 30 min

PREMIUMS

An advertising promotion that began in the early years of radio was the incentive of premiums to enhance the sales of the sponsor's product. In ex-change for box tops, product labels, or the backs of cereal packages -- along perhaps with ten or 25 cents to cover the cost of mailing and handling -- all sorts of premiums were offered that appealed specially to young listeners.

The LITTLE ORPHAN ANNIE show that ran from 1930 to 1942 led the way with merchandising gimmicks that included membership in a secret society with decoder pins, rings and badges, a shake-up mug (for the show's initial sponsor, Ovaltine), photos of the cast, and even a sheet music copy of the show's theme music.

Radio Orphan Annie (ROA). Secret Society Decoder Badge

Other shows like CAPTAIN MIDNIGHT followed suite with secret societies, manuals, decoders, membership certificates and incentives that lured the juvenile audience with whistles, periscopes, maps, magnifying glasses and pedometers. The decoding devices allowed listeners to decipher a secret message at the show's end usually previewing an upcoming episode. Rings were especially popular with secret compartments, sirens, and mirrors for looking backwards.

THE LONE RANGER, not to be left in the dust, offered a ring surmounted by a miniature six-shooter that actually shot sparks. Among the many premiums from the Masked Rider of the Plains were pop-guns, deputy badges and items emblazoned with silver bullets.

One personal favorite from THE SHADOW was a ring that glowed in the dark after being exposed to bright light. How many hours were spent by children in dark closets fascinated by the eerie glow of that luminous plastic ring.

The war years had their influence as premium material changed from copper, tin and brass to paper items. There were cardboard model planes and walkie-talkies, military insignia, devices for junior bombardiers that released toy bombs on imaginary axis targets, as well as blackout kits and "plane spotters" that silhouetted allied and enemy aircraft.

Over the years of early radio, hundreds of novelties were offered. Today, premium collecting is a popular pastime with many items fetching high prices. The return for ten cents and a product label in the 1940s can now often demand several hundred dollars at antique shows and collector markets. If only those of us from the radio years had known!

SOME MEMORABLE LINES

For listeners of early radio shows, who could forget these immortal lines:

The Shadow: Who knows what evil lurks in the hearts of men -- the weed of crime bears bitter fruit -- crime does not pay -- the Shadow knows.

The Lone Ranger: Return with us now to those thrilling days of yesteryear. From out of the past come the thundering hoofbeats of the great horse Silver! A fiery horse with the speed of light, a cloud of dust and a hearty Hi-Yo Silver! The Lone Ranger Rides again!

The Whistler: I am the Whistler, and I know many things, for I walk by night. I know many strange tales, many secrets hidden in the hearts of men and women who have stepped into the shadows. Yes, I know the nameless terrors of which they dare not speak ...

The Adventures of Superman: Faster than a speeding bullet! More powerful than a locomotive! Able to leap tall buildings at a single bound! Look! Up in the sky! It's a bird! It's a plane! It's Superman!

The Red Skelton Show: The character Junior, aka "the mean whiddle kid" was always contemplating some kind of mischief. If I dood it I get a whipping. Throwing caution to the wind, punishment sure to come, the deed was done, and Junior'd say, I dood it. I dood it again.

Gunsmoke: The story of the violence that moved west with young America, and the story of a man who moved with it. I'm that man, Matt Dillon, United States Marshall, the first man they look for, and the last man they want to meet.

The Great Gildersleeve: Peavey, the druggist, would always counter assertions with, "Well now, I wouldn't say that, Mr. Gildersleeve."

The Bob Hope Show: Being a former Marine myself, I enjoyed Hope's comment of how he found the Quantico Marine Base. I just drove down US 1 and turned left at the first craps game.

SIGNATURE SONGS

Most of radio's top performers had a signature song – one by which they were readily identified -- and these songs were occasionally the theme song for their show. Let's take a look at a few.

Kate Smith	When the Moon Comes Over the Mountain God Bless America
Bing Crosby	When the Blue of the Night Meets the Gold of the Day
Jimmy Durante	Inka-Dinka Doo
Rudy Vallee	My Time Is Your Time, The Wiffenpoof Song
Arthur Godfrey	Seems Like Old Times
Bob Hope	Thanks for the Memory
Eddie Cantor	Ida (Sweet as Apple Cider)
Al Jolson	April Showers, My Mammy, Swanee
Gene Autry	Back in the Saddle Again
Roy Rogers	Happy Trails

But not all signature songs became theme songs. These for example:

George Burns	Ain't Misbehavin'
Phil Harris	That's What I Like About the South
Jack Benny	Love in Bloom

Besides being identified with performers, songs were also linked to celebrities and cast characters. *Arkansas Traveler* brought an image of Edgar Bergen's rube dummy Mortimer Snerd. *Some Day I'll Find You* was the theme song for MR. KEEN, TRACER OF LOST PERSONS. The President of the United States was always accompanied by *Hail to the Chief*.

Along with signature songs there were signature catchphrases like Joe Penner's "Wanna buy a duck?" and Red Skelton's Junior -- the mean widdle kid -- "If I dood it I gets a licking." Or Superman's taking flight with "Up, up and away!" The Lone Ranger's "Hi-Yo, Silver!" Lou Costello's "I'm a baaad boy" and "Hey! Abbott!" From the ALDRICH FAMILY show: "Hen-ree! Henry Aldrich!" And Henry's cracked voice response: "Coming, Mother!" Not to be outdone, Bob and Ray had a mythical character in their show's credit lines whose name was like a Swiss yodel: O. Leo Lahey. Roy Roger's show closing sign-off was "Goodbye, good luck, and may the good Lord take a likin' to ya."

ON THE AIR

Old-time Radio, often referred to as OTR, is still very much alive today. On the web, *Archive.org* recaptures in their entirety hundreds of early shows. Satellite radio offers OTR 24/7. A number of shows have been syndicated and are back on the air again. My local NPR station offers a nightly weekday broadcast of old shows from 10 o'clock to midnight. Reenactment groups -- appropriately wearing clothes from the 30s and 40s and using original scripts -- act out episodes for theater audiences just as they were performed in those early radio studios. A nearby high school has adapted the movie *It's A Wonderful Life* into a radio format and presents it online as it might have been broadcast in the 1940s.

With a variety of introductions – some musical, some not – and with an imaginary twist of the dial, we've seen that radio listeners could be transported to the Yukon, the old West, and the Land of Make Believe. They could fly high with Superman, Capt. Midnight, Hop Harrigan and Sky King or ride the ranges with Gene Autry, Tom Mix and, of course, the Lone Ranger. Yes, and be scared, thrilled, and horrified with shows like SUSPENSE, LIGHTS OUT and INNER SANCTUM, together with thrilling episodes of THE WHISTLER and THE MYSTERIOUS TRAVELER. For us it's been a fabulous trip down radio's Golden Years and a well deserved salute to radio's "Theater of the Mind." We've seem how pictures could be painted with the brush strokes of words and music. Indeed, the pickings were great, the music memorable.

And now – instead of organ music that was a mainstay for innumerable early shows – we've arranged many of these themes for you to play on the ukulele. Imagine yourself in a radio studio playing a show's theme and scene music. Create an audio podcast and put together your own radio-style show with original episodes and theme music of your own choosing, old or new. Or, just take any one of the songs presented in this book and enjoy it for its own sake.

And like the opening words of THE LONE RANGER: "Return with us now to those thrilling days of yesteryear ..." Let your imagination run free. Discover for yourself what's old is truly new again.

SONGS IN LOW G TUNING

THEME SONG	PROGRAM
Juanita	The Romance of Helen Trent
Oh! You Beautiful Doll	Vic and Sade
Poor Butterfly	Myrt and Marge
Rock-a-Bye Baby	The Baby Snooks Show
The Kerry Dance	Portia Faces Life

LOW G TUNING: In this tuning the 4th string is dropped an octave lowering it from a High G to a Low G. The tuning is GCEA. Songs whose range would otherwise require playing the upper frets can now be arranged more easily on the lower frets. Songs can still be played in standard tuning but the 4th string notes will sound an octave higher than usual. Listen to the online audio to hear the correct pitch.

RADIO MUSIC THEMES AND THEIR SHOWS

April Showers	Kraft Music Hall
Arkansas Traveler	Bob Burns Show
Believe Me If All Those Endearing Young Charms	Aunt Jenny's Real-Life Stories
Bury Me Not on the Lone Pairie	Red Ryder
California, Here I Come	George Jessel Show
Charley, My Boy	Spike Jones Show
Columbia, The Gem of the Ocean	Don Winslow of the Navy
Darling Nelly Gray	Just Plain Bill
Eyes of Texas, The	Tales of the Texas Rangers
For He's A Jolly Good Fellow	Henry Morgan Show
Funiculi, Funicula	Lorenzo Jones
Hot Time in the Old Town Tonight	National Barn Dance
Ida! Sweet As Apple Cider	Eddie Cantor Shows
I've Been Working on the Railroad	Railroad Hour
Jimmy Crack Corn	Burl Ives Shows
Juanita	Romance of Helen Trent
Kerry Dance	Portia Faces Life
Love Nest	Burns & Allen Show
Memories	Stella Dallas
Merrily We Roll Along	Truth or Consequences
My Wild Irish Rose	Abie's Irish Rose
Nobody's Sweetheart	Joan Davis Show
Oh! You Beautiful Doll	Vic and Sade Show
On the Trail of the Lonesome Pine	Arthur Godfrey Time
Piano Concerto, No. 1 (Tchaikovsky)	Mercury Theater of the Air
Poor Butterfly	Myrt and Marge Show
Pop! Goes the Weasel	Vox Pop
Red River Valley	Our Gal Sunday
Rock-a-bye Baby	Baby Snooks Show
Rose Room	Phil Harris & Alice Faye Show
School Days	Quiz Kids
Sidewalks of New York	Horn & Hardart Children's Hour
Sunbonnet Sue	David Harum
When Irish Eyes Are Smiling	Duffy's Tavern
Yankee Doodle Boy	Jack Benny Show
Year of Jubilo	Edgar Bergen & Charlie McCarthy Show

SOME RADIO SHOWS AND THEIR MUSIC THEMES

Abie's Irish Rose	My Wild Irish Rose
Arthur Godfrey Show	On the Trail of the Lonesome Pine
Aunt Jenny's Real-Life Stories	Believe Me If All Those Endearing Young Charms
Baby Snooks Show	Rock-a-Bye Baby
Bob Burns Show	Arkansas Traveler
Burl Ives Show	Jimmy Crack Corn
Burns & Allen Show	Love Nest
David Harum	Sunbonnet Sue
Dick Tracy	Toot Toot Tootsie
Don Winslow of the Navy	Columbia, the Gem of the Ocean
Duffy's Tavern	When Irish Eyes Are Smiling
Eddie Cantor Show	Ida! Sweet As Apple Cider
Edgar Bergen & Charlie McCarthy Show	Year of Jubilo
George Jessel Show	California, Here I Come
Henry Morgan Show	For He's A Jolly Good Fellow
Horn & Hardart Children's Hour	Sidewalks of New York
Jack Benny Show	Yankee Doodle Boy
Joan Davis Show	Nobody's Sweetheart
Just Plain Bill	Darling Nelly Gray
Kraft Music Hall	April Showers
Lorenzo Jones	Funiculi, Funicula
Mercury Theater of the Air	Piano Concerto, No. 1 (Tchaikovsky)
Myrt & Marge Show	Poor Butterfly
National Barn Dance	Hot Time in the Old Town Tonight
Our Gal Sunday	Red River Valley
Phil Harris & Alice Faye Show	Rose Room
Portia Faces Life	Kerry Dance
Quiz Kids	School Days
Railroad Hour	I've Been Working on the Railroad
Red Ryder	Bury Me Not on the Lone Prairie
Romance of Helen Trent	Juanita
Spike Jones Show	Charley, My Boy
Stella Dallas	Memories
Tales of the Texas Rangers	The Eyes of Texas
Truth or Consequences	Merrily We Roll Along
Vic & Sade Show	Oh! You Beautiful Doll
Vox Pop	Pop! Goes the Weasel

KRAFT MUSIC HALL

April Showers

Buddy DeSilva

Louis Silvers

Ukulele tuning: gCEA

Though A - pril show - ers__ may come your way,__ they bring the flow - ers__ that bloom in May,__ so if it's rain - ing,__ have no re - grets__ be - cause it is - n't rain - ing rain you know it's rain - ing vi - o - lets. And when you

18

THE BOB BURNS SHOW

Arkansas Traveler

Ukulele tuning: gCEA

Traditional

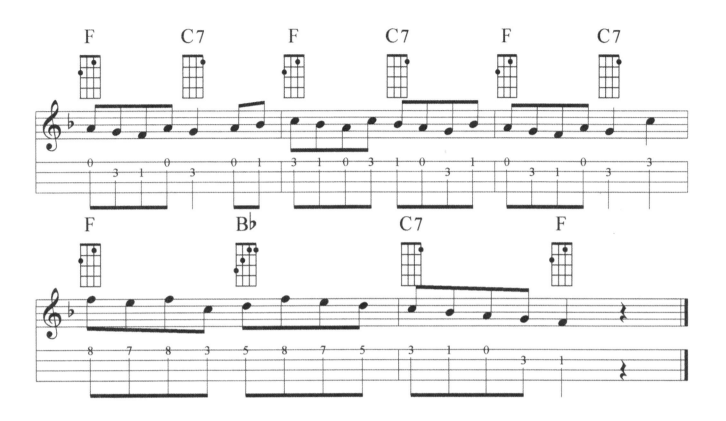

AUNT JENNY'S REAL-LIFE STORIES

Believe Me If All Those Endearing Young Charms

Ukulele tuning: gCEA

Thomas Moore

RED RYDER

Bury Me Not On The Lone Prairie

Ukulele tuning: gCEA

Traditional

RED RYDER

25

2. "Oh, bury me not," and his voice failed there,
But they took no heed of his dying prayer.
In a narrow grave, just six by three,
There buried him there on the lone prairie.

3. "Oh, bury me not on the lone prairie
Where the coyotes howl and the wind blows free,
Where there's not a soul who will care for me,
Oh, bury me not on the lone prairie."

GEORGE JESSEL SHOW

California, Here I Come

Ukulele tuning: gCEA

Al Jolson, B.G.deSilva, Joseph Meyer

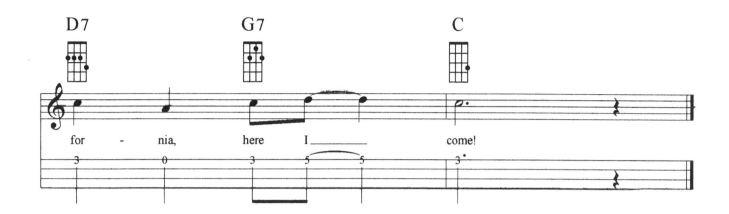

for - nia,   here   I _____ come!

SPIKE JONES SHOW

Charley My Boy

Ted Fiorito

Gus Kahn

Ukulele tuning: gCEA

Char-ley my boy, Oh Char-ley my boy, you thrill me, you chill me, with shiv-ers of joy,

you got that kind-a, sort-a, bit of a way, that makes me, takes me, tell me what shall I say.

And when we dance I read in your glance, whole pag-es and ag-es of love and ro-mance,

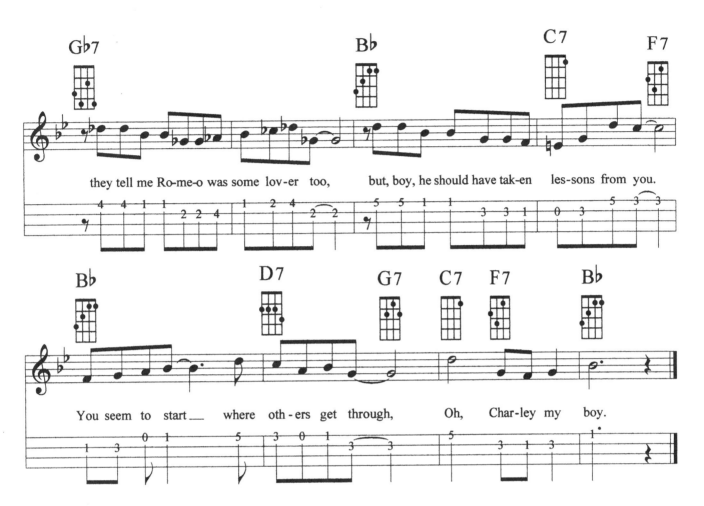

they tell me Ro-me-o was some lov-er too, but, boy, he should have tak-en les-sons from you.

You seem to start___ where oth-ers get through, Oh, Char-ley my boy.

Spike Jones & his City Slickers

DON WINSLOW OF THE NAVY

Columbia, The Gem of the Ocean

Ukulele tuning; gCEA

David T. Shaw

DON WINSLOW OF THE NAVY

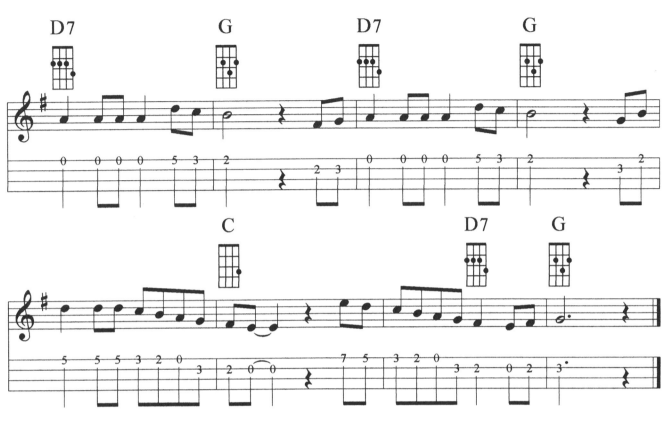

JUST PLAIN BILL

Darling Nelly Gray

Ukulele tuning: gCEA

B.R. Hanby

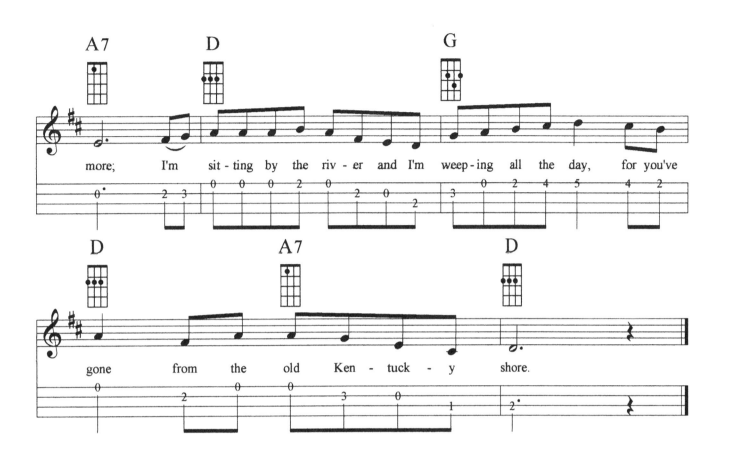

more; I'm sit - ting by the riv - er and I'm weep - ing all the day, for you've

gone from the old Ken - tuck - y shore.

TALES OF THE TEXAS RANGERS

The Eyes of Texas

Ukulele tuning: gCEA

Traditional melody

LORENZO JONES

Funiculi Funicula

Ukulele tuning: gCEA

Luigi Denza

This lively Italian musical theme is one section of a three-part song that commemorates the first funicular cable car on Mount Vesuvius. The title means "Funicular up, Funicular down."

HENRY MORGAN SHOW

For He's A Jolly Good Fellow

Ukulele tuning: gCEA

Traditional

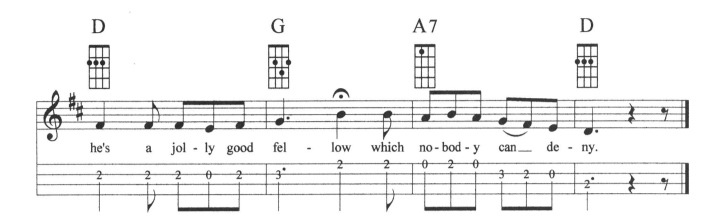

NATIONAL BARN DANCE

There'll Be A Hot Time In The Old Town Tonight
Ukulele tuning: gCEA

Joe Hayden

Theo. A Metz

BURL IVES SHOWS

Jimmy Crack Corn

Ukulele tuning: gCEA

Traditional

EDDIE CANTOR SHOWS

Ida! Sweet As Apple Cider

Ukulele tuning: gCEA

Eddie Leonard

THE RAILROAD HOUR
I've Been Working On The Railroad

Ukulele tuning: gCEA

Traditional

THE RAILROAD HOUR

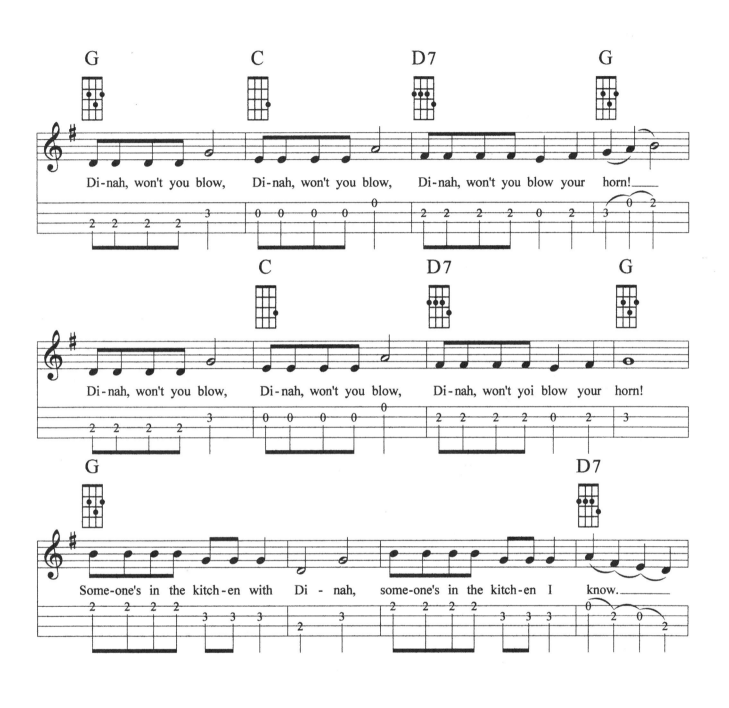

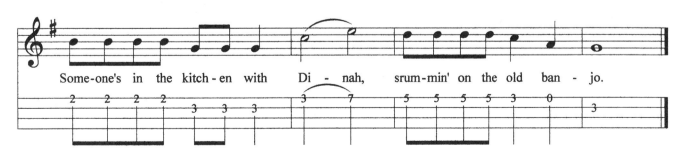

THE ROMANCE OF HELEN TRENT

Juanita

Ukulele in Low G tuning: GCEA

Traditional

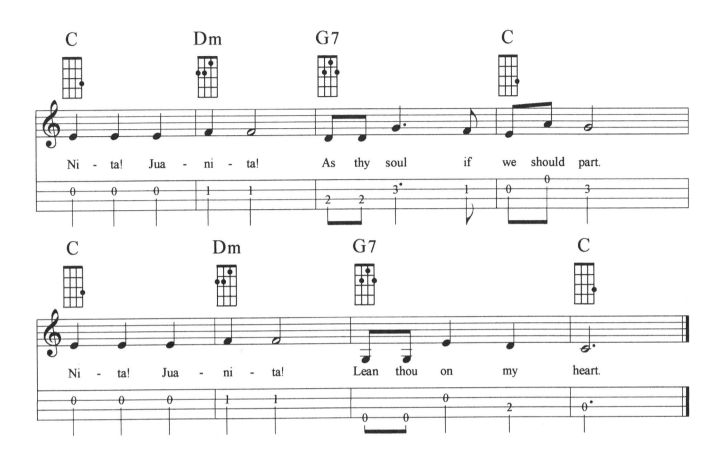

C   Dm   G7   C

Ni - ta! Jua - ni - ta! As thy soul if we should part.

C   Dm   G7   C

Ni - ta! Jua - ni - ta! Lean thou on my heart.

45

PORTIA FACES LIFE

The Kerry Dance

Ukulele in Low G tuning: GCEA

James L. Molloy

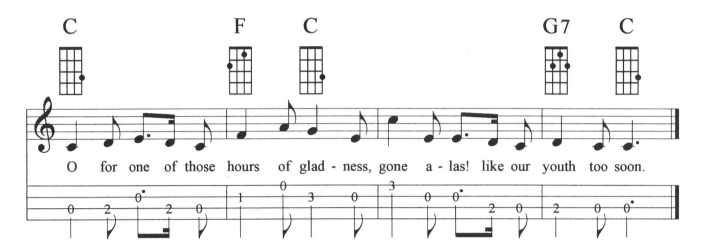

O for one of those hours of glad - ness, gone a - las! like our youth too soon.

STELLA DALLAS

Memories

Ukulele tuning: gCEA

Gus Kahn

Egbert Van Alstyne

THE BURNS & ALLEN SHOW
The Love Nest

Ukulele tuning: gCEA

Louis Hirsch

TRUTH OR CONSEQUENCES

Merrily We Roll Along

Ukulele tuning: gCEA

Traditional

JOAN DAVIS TIME

Nobody's Sweetheart

Ukulele tuning: gCEA

Gus Kahn & Ernie Erdman

Billy Meyers & Elmer Schoebel

ABIE'S IRISH ROSE

My Wild Irish Rose

Ukulele tuning: gCEA

Chauncey Olcott

ABIE'S IRISH ROSE

VIC AND SADE SHOW

Oh! You Beautiful Doll

Ukulele Low G tuning: GCEA

Seymour Brown

Nat D Ayer

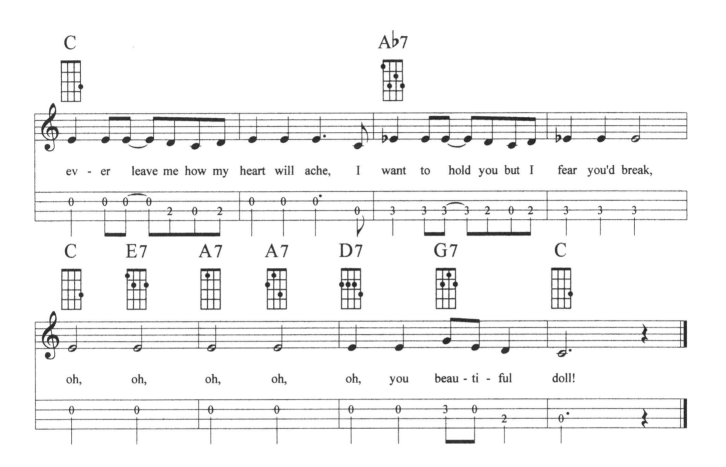

C   **A♭7**

ev - er leave me how my heart will ache, I want to hold you but I fear you'd break,

C **E7** **A7** **A7** **D7** **G7** **C**

oh, oh, oh, oh, oh, you beau - ti - ful doll!

ARTHUR GODFREY TIME

On The Trail of the Lonesome Pine

Ukulele tuning: gCEA

Ballard MacDonald

Harry Carroll

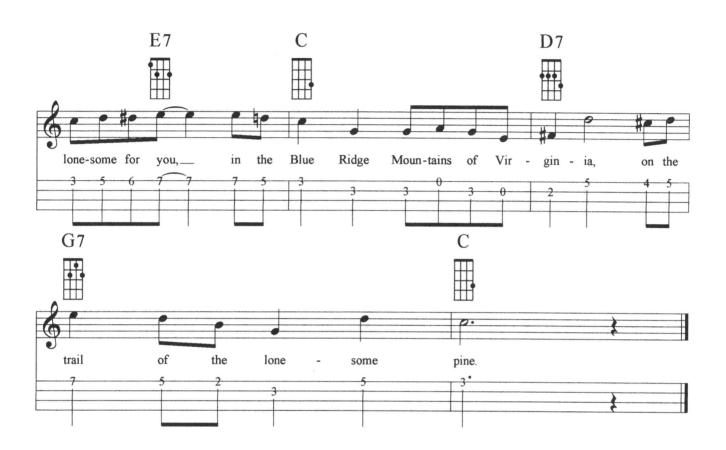

E7　　　　　C　　　　　　　　D7

lone-some for you,___ in the Blue Ridge Moun-tains of Vir - gin - ia, on the

3　5　6　7　7　　7　5　　3　　　　3　　3　0　　3　0　　2　　5　　4　5

G7　　　　　　　　　　　　C

trail　of　the　lone - some　pine.

7　　5　2　　　　3　　5　　　3

MERCURY THEATER OF THE AIR

Piano Concerto, No. 1

Ukulele tuning: gCEA

PYOTR ILYITCH TCHAIKOVSKY

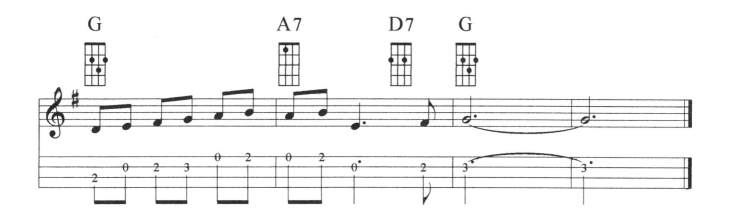

MYRT AND MARGE SHOW

Poor Butterfly

Ukulele in Low G tuning: GCEA

John L. Golden

Raymond Hubbell

MYRT AND MARGE SHOW

Inspired by the unrequited love theme of Giacomo Puccini's opera "Madama Butterfly."

VOX POP

Pop! Goes The Weasel

Ukulele tuning: gCEA

Traditional

OUR GAL SUNDAY

Red River Valley

Ukulele tuning: gCEA

Traditional

From this val - ley they say you are go - ing, ___ we will
Come and sit by my side if you love me. ___ Do not

miss your bright eyes and sweet smile, for they
has - ten to bid me a - dieu, just re -

say you are tak - ing the sun - shine ___ that has
mem - ber the Red Riv - er Val - ley ___ and the

bright - ened our path - ways a - while.
cow - boy who loved you so true.

THE BABY SNOOKS SHOW

Rock-A-Bye Baby

Ukulele in Low G tuning: GCEA

Traditional

DAVID HARUM

Sunbonnet Sue

Ukulele tuning: gCEA

Will D. Cobb

Gus Kahn

PHIL HARRIS/ALICE FAYE SHOW

Rose Room

Ukulele tuning: gCEA

Harry Williams

Art Hickham

QUIZ KIDS

School Days

Ukulele tuning: gCEA

Gus Edwards

HORN & HARDART CHILDREN'S HOUR

The Sidewalks of New York

Ukulele tuning: gCEA

JAMES W. BLAKE
CHARLES B. LAWLOR

DICK TRACY

Toot, Toot, Tootsie

Ukulele tuning: gCEA

Gus Kahn

TOOT TOOT TOOTSIE

TOOT TOOT TOOTSIE

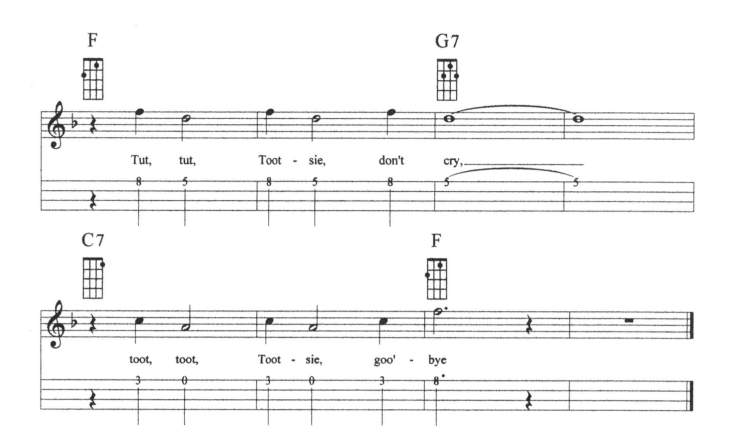

Tut, tut, Toot - sie, don't cry,

toot, toot, Toot - sie, goo' - bye

EDGAR BERGEN & CHARLIE McCARTHY SHOW

Year of Jubilo

Ukulele tuning: gCEA

Henry Clay Work

DUFFY'S TAVERN

When Irish Eyes Are Smiling

Ukulele tuning: gCEA

Chauncey Olcott et al.

THE JACK BENNY SHOW
The Yankee Doodle Boy

Ukulele tuning: gCEA

George M. Cohan

More Great Ukulele Books from Centerstream...

CHRISTMAS UKULELE, HAWAIIAN STYLE

Play your favorite Christmas songs Hawaiian style with expert uke player Chika Nagata. This book/CD pack includes 12 songs, each played 3 times: the first and third time with the melody, the second time without the melody so you can play or sing along with the rhythm-only track. Songs include: Mele Kalikimaka (Merry Christmas to You) • We Wish You a Merry Christmas • Jingle Bells (with Hawaiian lyrics) • Angels We Have Heard on High • Away in a Manger • Deck the Halls • Hark! The Herald Angels Sing • Joy to the World • O Come, All Ye Faithful • Silent Night • Up on the Housetop • We Three Kings.

00000472 Book/CD Pack $19.95

FUN SONGS FOR UKULELE

INCLUDES TAB

50 terrific songs in standard notation and tablature for beginning to advanced ukulele players. Includes Hawaiian songs, popular standards, classic Western, Stephen Foster and more, with songs such as: The Darktown Strutters Ball • I'm Always Chasing Rainbows • Hot Lips • Gentle Annie • Maikai Waipio • Whispering • Ja-Da • China Boy • Colorado Trail • and many more. Also includes a chord chart and a special section on how to hold the ukulele.

00000407... $14.95

ULTIMATE LIT'L UKULELE CHORDS, PLUS

INCLUDES TAB

by Kahuna Uke (aka Ron Middlebrook)

This handy 6' x 9' guide in the popular C tuning provides all the ukulele chords you'll ever need or use. The diagrams are easy to use and follow, with all the principal chords in major and minor keys, in all the different chords positions. Plus, there are sections on How to Begin, Scales on All Strings, Note Studies, and Chord Modulations (great to use for intros & endings!). This handy 32 page guide fits right in a case perfectly. Happy strumming, you'll Mahalo me latter.

00001351... $7.99

ASAP UKULELE

INCLUDES TAB

Learn How to Play the Ukulele Way

by Ron Middlebrook

This easy new method will teach you the ukulele ASAP! Each exercise in the book has been designed to teach you the most popular key chord combinations and patterns that you'll see in hundreds of songs. The tunes taught here include: Auld Lang Syne - My Bonnie Lies Over the Ocean - Oh! Susanna - Peg of My Heart - Red River Valley - Tiger Rag - and many more. You can strum the chords for each, or play the easy-to-follow melody.

00001359... $14.99

KEV'S QUICKSTART FINGERSTYLE UKULELE

INCLUDES TAB

by Kevin Rones

Go Beyond Three Chords And A Strum!
This book/CD package is for anyone who want to become better at playing the ukulele.

Newbies: Have fun learning how to play Fingerstyle Ukulele quickly without having to read music! **Ukulele Strummers:** Tired of strumming the same old chords? This book will have you picking in no time! **Indie Artist and Songwriters:** Expand you song writing and performance with Fingerstyle Ukulele. **Guitars players:** If you already play guitar this book is your shortcut into learning Ukulele. Learn arrangements written specifically for Fingerstyle Ukulele: Bach, Blues, Folk, Celtic and more!

000001590... $17.99

UKULELE FOR COWBOYS

INCLUDES TAB

40 of your favorite cowboy songs in chords, standard notation and tab. Includes: Buffalo Gals • Night Herding Song • Doney Gal • Old Chisholm Trail • The Big Corral • Ragtime Cowboy Joe • Colorado Trail • Old Paint • Yellow Rose of Texas • Green Grow the Lilacs • and many more. Also includes a chord chart, historical background on many of the songs, and a short story on the history of the Hawaiian Cowboy.

00000408... $14.99

UKULELE SONGBOOK

INCLUDES TAB

compiled by Ron Middlebrook

This terrific collection for beginning to advanced ukulele players features easy arrangements of 50 great songs, in standard notation and tablature. Also teaches popular strum patterns, and how to tune the uke.

00000248... $9.95

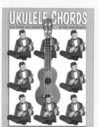

UKULELE CHORDS

Plus Intros and Endings

by Ron Middlebrook

This handy chart includes clear, easy-to-see chord fingerings in all keys, plus a bonus section that provides favorite intros and endings in different keys. Also includes information on relative tuning.

00000246... $2.95

SONGS OF THE CIVIL WAR FOR UKULELE

by Dick Sheridan

25 tunes of the era that boosted morale, championed causes, pulled on the heartstrings, or gave impetus to battle. Includes: All Quiet Along the Potomac, Aura Lee, Battle Hymn of the Republic, Dixie, The Girl I Left Behind Me, John Brown's Body, When Johnny Comes Marching Home and more - all in standard C tuning, with notation, tablature and accompanying lyrics. The book also includes notes on the songs, historical commentary, and a handy chord chart!

00001588... $14.99

THE LOW G STRING TUNING UKULELE

INCLUDES TAB

by Ron Middlebrook

25 popular songs for the ukulele in standard music notation, tablature and easy chords. To get the most out of this book, you'll want to replace the fourth (high G) string with one of a heavier gauge and tune it an octave lower to get that full, deep sound – a lá Hawaiian uke virtuoso Jesse Kalima – in playing the melodies in this book. The chords can be played with or without the low G sound.

00001534 Book/CD Pack $19.99

P.O. Box 17878 - Anaheim Hills, CA 92817
(714) 779-9390   www.centerstream-usa.com